ELEGY FOR AN APPETITE

SHAINA LOEW-BANAYAN

[PANK]BOOKS

Cover design by Sasha Ori

Library of Congress Cataloging-in-Publication Data

ISBN 978-1-948587-25-9

PANK Magazine
PANK Books

To purchase multiple copies or book events, readings and author signings contact awesome@pankmagazine.com.

ELEGY FOR AN APPETITE

SHAINA LOEW-BANAYAN

FOR ANYONE WHO MIGHT
WANT IT

Contents

PART I

JONNY 1

RAZE 2

BABY GRAND 3

GRAND BABY 4

FAT BUTT 5

DEATH OF BOWL CUT 7

JUICY 8

PEEPING TOM 9

FRANK (HORSE IN THE STYLE OF COCOON) 10

HOUNDSTOOTH 11

QUARTER-SLICE 13

SPOONS 14

& THE MOUTH IS PLEASED 15

BOW 16

DR. BALLERINA 17

PART II

NEW YORK CITY BABY 19

ROUTE SEVENTEEN SOUTH 20

SOUS VIDE TECHNOLOGY... 21

THE ROUTINE 22

CARROT TARTARE 23

CHEF..24

OUI (EMPEROR'S CLOTHING)... 25

SERVICE SHIFT..26

SERVICE SHIFT II (SHOW DUCK) 27

GROCERY THIEF, ETC. 29

JERZ 31

POTATOES INSIDE YOUR ACTUAL SHOE..................................... 32

LAYING STONE... 33

BROWN...34

BISCUITS 35

THE GOOD FOOD.. 37

CHURCH GUY 39

YOU SHOULD NOT PUSH YOUR SLOWER FRIEND DOWN TO
SAVE YOURSELF FROM THE BEAR... 40

IF YOU ARE PACKING VAG YOU COULD WALK INTO A
KITCHEN HOLDING A HEAD ON A SPIKE & THE PREPUBES-
CENT FIRST DAY INTERN WOULD TELL YOU A BETTER WAY
TO SHOW OFF YOUR BOUNTY. 41

PART III

PANTIES 45

AT THE SILLY GOOSE 47

SPLINTER 48

GOING PLACES 50

SAP 51

THE GRAM 53

MOOD BOARD 55

THIRD FLOOR 56

KNIFE GUY 57

FRYER OIL 58

ENDER: PURPOSE 59

LEAP YEAR 61

SHIT SHOOTING 63

PICTURE A MOUNTAIN 64

PART IV: Epilogue

THE PRESENT POETIC 67

ELEGY FOR AN APPETITE

SHAINA LOEW-BANAYAN

PART I

Jonny

THE FIRST CHEF I ever worked for was a guy named Jonny had yellow buck teeth with a gap in the middle age forty-something already had gout bad peripheral vision always bumping into things. Huge fan of poop humor talked nonstop of his days at Chez Catherine out in California loved harassing the dishwasher loved harassing his sous chef harmless overall just high-pitched-cackle annoying as hell. He couldn't keep it together about anything, would waste time pondering great philosophical conundra between bleats of laughter like:

WHAT DO I DO if I stay at a friend's house and they give me a washcloth for the shower do I wash my ass with the cloth or just give it back dry and they think I didn't wash at all.

FOOD WAS DECENT SUPER old school every other word he said was demi glace but he had a hard lisp so it sounded like demi glath. Crocs the size of boats. Sausage finger hands. Boyish haircut tinged with innocence like he accidentally climbed up a beanstalk walked into this kitchen & never found his way out.

Raze

I WAS FIFTEEN YEARS old wasn't into much other than hating the world and cooking. Food was always a joy never a nuisance I had tired of humans but certainly not of cake. To be honest though what I hadn't tired of was the idea of cake the eating of it was a separate issue I had crawled into a snare of anorexia never ate much cake no never much of anything at all. By then I'd crept back under one hundred wed in solemn matrimony to my bones & numbers that started in nine & once in a moon even eight I never spoiled myself with the squareness of a meal but fed my spirit on the fumes of what I cooked for my parents and siblings. As I subsisted on raw calculations I concocted for them everything I longed to taste & in this time I taught myself to cook. How I loved to bake cakes even if eating them was forbidden I could certainly be near them next to them touching them & oh to watch the ripples in the batter as the beaters twisted fast to see the layers swell over pan rims in the oven to be accosted by vanilla and butter in the air to turn out the tender sponges raze their domes and frost them hidden into cake glorious cake. To foist it on my family.

Baby Grand

TO WORSHIP STARVING AND cooking side by side was to dance compulsively around a circle of longing and loathing but we don't always consider those things before apprenticing ourselves to the mind's twitching jigsaw. So food in all its splendor retained a certain evil & my hunger made me mean. Superior too I kept my judgments of everybody else churning just below the surface or sometimes stashed between piano key ribs. Piano, piano. That's just something my mom said one day back then when she hugged me. *I can play your ribs like a piano.* Don't misunderstand the context though it was not a joke it was a sigh if anything. The kind of sigh you make when you embrace a person you once hotly birthed and she is all ice wood & ivory.

Grand Baby

BEFORE THAT THOUGH I was a ravenous child liked eating loved eating always wanted more. More dinner more play more costumes I lived inside the palm burn of monkey bars loved impressing the babysitter loved scaring the babysitter I ate clementines whole ate everything whole climbed door jambs to the molding slap & then jumped. In Hebrew school my favorite part was snack time we had challah & we had grape juice & when we said the bracha everyone put their hands on the bread & ripped it apart at amen. I had it all worked out when the teacher brought the challah & we circled around it *baruch atah adonai* I reached out my hand *eloheinu melech ha'olam* put my palm on one braid-lump *hamotzi lechem* while stretching each finger as far as possible over the surrounding territory *min ha'aretz* my peers were not as ambitious *we give thanks to god for bread* I gripped hard *amen* twisted my hand pulled fast & scored something like a quarter loaf all for myself. The crust was burnished sweet the ropey dough collapsed even denser as I chewed I washed it down with urgent gulps of Manischewitz grape juice & God was a plausible creature. Amen amen amen.

Fat Butt

WILKE'S DELICATESSEN WAS AROUND the corner and down the street from the house we were renting in Ridgewood the year I turned nine. Everyone else's shitty convenience store was my Valhalla my red razor scooter my steed & Hostess cakes my feast. Yodels were my favorite but anything chocolate was worth trying & cream filling was the only hard criterion. One most victorious day I rushed home from Wilke's to brag to my mom about scoring Devil Dogs at a three-for-two price. *You know you really shouldn't eat so many snacks* is what she said. *You're getting chubby.* Chubby chubby I didn't know chubby only the sturdiness of my appetite and of course my impressive strength. But chubby began to stalk me like a shadow does just nipping at your heels as though if you stop moving it'll consume you & even if you don't it might swoop around and face you anyway at the fickle whim of the sun. At my birthday party a girl told me that the whipped cream on my ice cream sundae would make my butt fat. I don't think I really knew what that meant or that I even had a butt but I could tell that a Fat Butt was very bad. Lo just as sure as I was infatuated with Reddi-wip the scourge of The Fat Butt came true: I was damned to calling to my mom for larger shorts from the dressing room at Limited Too & at sewing class I even had to exit the fitting room with my pants stuck halfway down my legs, Fat Butt refusing the pattern made for everybody else. *Well* Mrs. Faucet had said *we are all out of the denim why don't you choose something else we'll rip out the side seams & add in some panels.* While the rest of the class primly ironed their monochromes, I turned, orange Hawaiian print in hand, toward whatever fate awaits the one who trespasses on the sanctity of bluejean.

Death of Bowl Cut

AS WELL AS BEING chubby I was guilty of being what we used to call a tomboy & that became less adorable as I neared puberty. I liked short hair something about it just felt right plus we were living in the time of Nick Carter & bowl cuts were a thing that normal people did to their heads very much on purpose the only problem was that of those normal people chopping their hair short at such a singular and decisive latitude the vast majority were boys. But I was in a time of not comparing myself to the other girls I just was & they were & it was the world. By the time I was ten though I was made to grow out my bowl cut & even though I didn't know why or agree I relented. As my hair grew I watched it pass my earlobes in the mirror & my mom said you look so pretty with your hair pulled back & she put it in half-up-half-down. All I could really know about it was that Orlando Bloom wore his hair like this in *Pirates* & so maybe I looked like him. I didn't have any type of goatee of course but it was something of an optimism. The other girls at school had long hair very long hair & the more you were the same as them the more you had friends just like you & so I developed a certain gratitude for my lengthening blonde. But they were all skinny–long straight legs & chests that matched with any shirt– whereas I'd suddenly encountered boobs & pimples & a plateauing growth chart before I'd ever made it to my teen wardrobe prime.

Juicy

THE MINI SKIRT WAS the gold standard of Girl Outfit bottom-half choices. Shorts were fine pants were fine but did you have a Mini Skirt. My legs looked crazy in a short skirt they were all wrong with their hefty calves and Reddi-wip thighs that funneled awkwardly into knees that seemed to say Oh Fuck This rather than We Are Knees. But for me this was a fixable issue I had straight As & was a pretty quick study so once I'd tasted the fun-filled life of a long-haired pre-teen girl I was not about to let my shot at homogeneity slip away. A diet was to me nothing more than an extra credit project I simply had to learn how the fuck it worked plug in the variables & watch success happen. No more cookies no more junk food I hijacked my family's desktop to look up nutrition facts for hours learned the calories per gram of every food I ate apple .5 lettuce o butter 3 roast beef 1 I weighed my cereal before school I went grocery shopping with my mom switched to food products made of water some binders & some other crap things like fat free bologna, calorie-free dressing, *light* sandwich bread, chips fried in Olestra. I learned to make my own meals learned to disapprove of my family's eating habits & I even very charitably designed diet plans for my mother and sister. My daily minutes on our treadmill became hours marching toward the knobby knees of my peers. Toward the dress-code testing flounce of a Juicy Couture skirt in hot-pink terry.

Peeping Tom

BY AGE FIFTEEN I'D begun to swap out food for words and
pictures & my brain devoured information about all I desired to
eat but couldn't. I spent hours hunched over the computer stu-
pid-mouthed at tasting menus from places like Per Se & other
such kitchens where the courses went on and on and on. Thomas
you dirty boy say some more offal & more French shit. *Marrow.*
Sabayon, maybe. & the magazines. Have you ever tasted horny on
high-gloss photos of chicken thighs. O my Bon App centerfold.
That god color that sworn noise of teeth on breakable skin. & words
like deglaze that reach all the way into the cavernous colon. & how
I hung my week on the promise of Wednesdays with Frank Bruni
in the *New York Times* he told me the details of every bite every sip
every revelation & every failure. & in the afternoons I sat on the
large mustard-colored chair in our family room watching *Barefoot
Contessa* & *Thirty Minute Meals* & *Everyday Italian* wondering how
come Giada was so skinny did she really eat *padmeejiahno dejiano,*
mootsadell, pahnchaytah, pahnetohnay or did she just eat oatmeal
for breakfast a romaine salad no dressing for lunch maybe a diet
coke tell her family she already had dinner and then go to bed with

her knees resting hard on one another fearing she wouldn't wake up in the morning but fearing fatness so much more.

Frank (Horse in the Style of Cocoon)

THERE WAS MORE TO cooking than hangovers poop jokes & demi glace at least Frank Bruni implied so & I thought he was likely right. Something about how he made good food sound so godly & errors so criminal what he hated I hated too we just had this understanding. & the more I worshiped cooking the more Jonny seemed like a shit stain on the gleaming institution of Chefs. Bigger things were at hand you see it was time to be knowing about foams encapsulations and other such magics. Don't worry I was polite enough not to tell Jonny I was better than him. Just judged silently & let him think I was a pothead because I was tired from being cold from being skinny from being hungry from compulsively starving that kind of thing has a way of lulling you to sleep as in freezing to death, is often confused for being fully baked mellow but it really goes like this:

IMAGINE ALL THE RAGE of low blood sugar rolled up into a long tunnel and you look down the tunnel it doesn't have an end. Then the fatigue comes, hushing you into stillness, but mellow does not show up. You are grating potatoes for latkes everyone keeps leaving the back door open the winter's against your bones & your fingers go numb. It is so cold and your lips are blue. Are you dying? Maybe you can have a cup of tea. Or maybe a horse will split itself open in the middle of your frigid wasteland lay down in front of you get in. But you won't get into the horse. You'll lay down next to it.

Houndstooth

WINTER BREAK OF HIGH school junior year I arranged a pastry *stage* at wd~50 in Manhattan for two weeks–I am only telling you this restaurant because it is now closed & maybe it helps you know where we are on this map. *Stagier* is French for unpaid bitch & everyone knows that all great chefs start out as broke bitches. The kitchen was in a basement lit garish fluorescent had this smell about it that made me nervous not bad not good just maybe some type of soap and/or refrigerator. I showed up in torn jeans and a chef coat with a Wusthoff santoku inside a Bacardi bag my dad got for free at the liquor store & Chef said I bet you paid extra for the torn jeans & I said um & he said to the sous chef get her some pants. The pants they gave me were size medium black and white houndstooth made me look like I had shrunk in the wash & so the chef and sous chef fashioned me a belt out of plastic wrap & I tied the behemoth garment to my double zero waist. Chef said ok so cooking is work not fun. Jesus Christ what a douche I had thought in that moment but it didn't really matter either way I had tried his desserts they tasted so precise almost like he could hear the ingredients. Most people couldn't hear them too drunk too nourished & therefore too distracted but I was so hungry I never missed a note. In pastry at wd~50 we used razors to cut things instead of knives used meat glue to stick shit together passionfruit was still on trend foam was still the shit--it was the height of it all. Chef explained his ethos to me he said while our desserts were meant to be delicious they were also supposed to make other chefs think 'oh how clever what they did there how did they figure out how to do that.'

Quarter-Slice

ON THE NEW YEAR'S Eve of my *stage* we got pizza for staff meal & I sliced off a one-inch piece for myself I was not accustomed to eating meals daily whereas everyone else was normal & it was not a smooth thing to insist I was full. Another cook said don't be shy take more I could not but wanted to. Less for the pizza and more to be normal like them. Untethered. They were all cool as hell stampede fast but Led Zeppelin chill well everyone besides this sous chef he yelled when talking all round pupils and nostrils like staring at the sun too long & then away. What was it like to be these people I wanted to know they just marched off into the night after service hats coats and purpose like the life they were living was theirs & I resented my sixteenness my hunger my rules & even the state of New Jersey for being where I had to go. On the last night of my *stage* I begged my parents to go to Blue Ribbon Brasserie with me after service so we could eat dinner in the middle of the night like real cooks & they relented & we ate bone marrow with challah and matzoh ball soup at two in the morning. The following day, back on my hunger: who is the person that designs a mirage on the horizon of their own impossible.

Spoons

IN COLLEGE I GOT a job cooking at the hotel in my school my main job was banquets prep the food we made was I don't know like vinyl siding or a French manicure or a bed skirt & there's no other way to explain it I am sorry. We cut a lot of cheese plates I could never settle on pleasing geometric patterns I mean what is there to do with sage derby & what is the tasteful compromise between fanning crackers and fifty-two pickup. At work I tried not to taste but couldn't avoid it altogether & each time the calories pelted loud on my brain like grave dirt. The clean tasting spoons were upright in their *bain marie* the dirty ones faced down how many of the downward ones were mine & of those downward spoons how many were worth it probably none. On my dinner break in the cafeteria I had diet coke I was pleased by the way the soda chilled my bones not for the suffering but more for the reassurance that I lacked insulation. & if the caffeine made my hands sweat then nothing was cushioning it from my blood & if my rings hung loose on my fingers then I was less than I once had been. Mornings when I'd gained a pound or two I would call out of work for fear of the spoons & I never got in trouble because I was a student & our academics came first.

& the Mouth is Pleased

WHEN YOU ARE STARVING & then drink enough booze the hollow in you awakens & throws tantrums. Thursdays were for getting blackout in a bones-tight dress & then raccooning through dark fraternity kitchens in search of anything. Raiding lowboys, freezers, cabinets in primal scrounge for antitoxin. Frozen cookie dough tortilla chips leftover dinner whatever was there I was all mouth & everything tasted perfect. When you're gone you can't feel your insides & when you eat the brain stays good like cicadas in silent dusk. You just eat and eat and the mouth is pleased & the brain stays good & the guts don't know they are getting stuffed like sausages they just want to be filled and filled and filled. In the morning you realize you've ingested a restaurant sized bag of Tostitos & descend into the droughted purgatory of shame. Heart thumping mouth sharped guts clogged all you want is to unzip your skin & run out in just your bones. But there is no zipper.

Bow

MY BOYFRIEND NEVER KNEW anything much about my eating all he knew is how much I loved food & it is hard to be in love while starving oneself. Partially because starving survives on the isolation it requires to go unnoticed & partially because when faced with a sudden glut of happiness it is hard put a stop to it & snacks & drinks are implied in the wake of kissing laughing fucking adoring living. A starving body wants to grow it clings to sustenance just in case puts extras in its pockets against what it knows will happen again. So I grew & as I grew I drank and as I drank I ate and as I ate I loved and as I loved I grew and as I grew I drank and as I drank I ate and as I ate I loved and as I loved I grew & the growing was too fast & the drinking was not enough to obscure it & how else to appease my feral ache for the steadiness of clavicle. There is one last thing you say you'll never do & then you're bending over and it's not that hard. Stooping all the way down so far down that the taste sight smell of vomit in your mouth toilet nose invites revulsion but salvation shows up instead as the voices simmer away. & after all you are only bowing a little deeper to your gods & see how that demands a certain unexpected dedication.

Dr. Ballerina

*Well you **look** good* is what the doctor said when I arrived for
my appointment. I was nineteen & my mom had sent me to her
boss's therapist who specialized in ballerinas--ballerinas of course
being other people whose moms catch them puking up dinner while
visiting home. Well. you. *look.* good. said the ballerina specialist &
what he meant is when one looks good (& to whom?) one has no
reason to throw up a perfectly good braised short rib or (?) to go
to war with the body at all. *Aha* I said & left completely cured. Just
kidding that's not what happened I didn't know to just go home
when a therapist tells an anorexic bulimic patient You Look Good
so I stayed and he talked to me for a while & I cried a little & he
tried to make it about my dad but it wasn't & then he said *well you
can't be a chef if you can't get better.* & so I never went back & no
one made me. There eventually came the night my parents asked
if I was still puking I was rummaging around their fridge with my
back to them & I just said no more to the bottle of ketchup than
anyone else & changed topics. There is not a more flattening shame
than being asked these things it is worse than period staining the
couch in front of your dad worse than your mom finding a used
condom in your room worse than worse than worse. & it is true
that I tried to stop but jesus goddamn fuck is food everywhere
when you work in a kitchen & jesus goddamn fuck is it not allowed
the being of fat.

PART II

New York City Baby

THE BEST RESTAURANT IN The World had a kitchen at least forty times the size of Jonny's. Three walk-in refrigerators an entire room for dry storage an entire warehouse in the same building just for storing extra equipment plates props toys every seasonal menu needed a different set of these. Everyone wore a tall paper toque on their head & a long slate-blue apron. For the men it looked feasible for me I looked like a garden gnome which might be fine but the thing is that cooks become chefs garden gnomes stand in gardens & it is hard to be promoted when you're out standing with the rosemary no matter how square your brunoise. As well as your typical knife kit you had to have a pair of tweezers actually better to have one small and one long pair. No piercings no facial hair black socks only you had to wash your own three aprons for five days & you weren't allowed to be fat. We did the same thing every day ran around making everything we had into tiny cubes or purée or fluid gel--Jesus Christ the xanthan gum--sometimes you had to make so many types of gel you practically shit gel from tasting them day in and out. If you are not aware of xanthan gum it is a powder that turns any liquid into snot we made pear snot every day plum snot even sea urchin snot they made us blend our snots in the walk-in so the guests wouldn't hear the ingredients shrieking as they whizzed into slobbery jizz.

Route Seventeen South

I WAS COMMUTING TO the city from my parents' place in Jersey and was due into work by seven. I rode the first bus out at five twenty-seven AM which meant I violenced awake at least four times a night thinking I'd missed it. My first time at the bus stop the the driver swerved toward me stopped the vehicle so short it snorted and choked on its own saliva. *How am I supposed to see you if you don't shine a flashlight at me?* Well I didn't know there was an etiquette to this. There wasn't the bus was always late the driver didn't give a shit I once stood waiting in the dark as car after car ran over this fucking deer watched its limbs hack off into the navyness of December tuft by bloodied tuft. And when half an hour later the bus crested over that far belt of highway a cop pulled up to collect the carcass blocked the stop completely. Hey what the fuck I said. *Gotta get this deer but it's fine there's another bus in twenty minutes.*

Sous Vide Technology

IT WASN'T FINE MINUTES rode tight between my shoulders & I
just cried the whole way there. My minutes my minutes. The ones
I spent vacuum sealing carrots in plastic bags and writing all the
labels that said

12/3/2013 Carrots 7:23 AM 90 C
12/3/2013 Carrots 7:23 AM 90 C
12/3/2013 Carrots 7:23 AM 90 C
12/3/2013 Carrots 7:23 AM 90 C
12/3/2013 Carrots 7:23 AM 90 C
12/3/2013 Carrots 7:23 AM 90 C
12/3/2013 Carrots 7:23 AM 90 C
12/3/2013 Carrots 7:23 AM 90 C
12/3/2013 Carrots 7:23 AM 90 C
12/3/2013 Carrots 7:23 AM 90 C
12/3/2013 Carrots 7:23 AM 90 C
12/3/2013 Carrots 7:23 AM 90 C.
12/3/2013 Carrots 7:23 AM 90 C
12/3/2013 Carrots 7:23 AM 90 C
12/3/2013 Carrots 7:23 AM 90 C
12/3/2013 Carrots 7:23 AM 90 C
12/3/2013 Carrots 7:23 AM 90 C
12/3/2013 Carrots 7:23 AM 90 C
12/3/2013 Carrots 7:23 AM 90 C
12/3/2013 Carrots 7:23 AM 90 C

The Routine

I WAS IN CHARGE of the carrot tartare we each only got one or two dishes at a time & got stuck on them for weeks or even months either someone had to die or the season had to change for you to escape. Each day after bagging and steaming my carrots I'd cut bread on the bandsaw for toast points then I'd make plum mustard & then carrot vinaigrette then I'd get in a fight with Connor about how triangular the toast was or wasn't or with someone else about needing the blender then I'd slice chives and chef would throw them away & then I'd slice them again. Then I'd sort through sunflower seeds to make sure none of them was broken since goddamn motherfucking Connor used them all during dinner service last night & then I'd blend different juices with liquid nitrogen to make snows for the other *garde manger* dishes. Since we weren't allowed to reuse yesterday's *mise* every day was the same such that the tasks had to match the clock hands if you were three minutes behind you knew & if someone else caused it they knew.

Carrot Tartare

THIS DISH MADE THE *New York Times* it was a very big deal a very very big deal. During service I'd plate eleven condiments over and over again on a grid-shaped plate:

- carrot vinaigrette
- mustard oil
- quail egg yolk
- chives
- pickled mustard seeds
- dried bluefish

- plum mustard
- sunflower seeds
- diced plum
- fresh horseradish
- salt

AND SET UP TRAYS with bundles of the plastic-bag-cooked carrots which the *commis* team tied together in groups of two or three with their uncooked greens attached since we were playing pretend. For that course a server would attach a hand crank meat grinder to the guests' table then take out & present the carrot bundle grind it tableside & portion it onto the grid plates all smirk faced since it was not steak & the people they'd say stuff like oh what a clever jest. Next it was their job to decide on the best ratio of condiments to add to their paste. Some people used everything some people didn't the joy was more so in playing the tableside guacamole deity than in the actual eating of the thing.

Chef

CHEF LIKED TO YELL all the chefs liked to yell let's see there was King Chef, Chef, Executive Sous Chef, and then nine regular sous chefs above the thirty-something cooks. King Chef came by about twice a month in blinding chef whites and a Rolex his voice always whined like his mom just turned off the TV still he scared everyone he even scared Chef. Chef and Executive Sous ended every sentence with *Yeah* like hurry up, *yeah?* Let's hustle, *yeah?* That is a trick you do to force the person you're talking at to agree with you it is the British version of saying *OK?* At the Best Restaurants In The World you use language that is not American because it proves you were trained by someone who isn't a fuckwad. Once when King Chef came Chef made me hide the fat *stagier* in the kitchen of the private dining room *like he's Anne Frank, yeah?* if King Chef sees him he'll make him leave he hates fat people won't even let them trail never mind work.

Oui (Emperor's Clothing)

EVERY DAY BEFORE WE opened for service Chef gave a speech and we all had to shout *Oui!* at the end in order to make him think we thought what we were doing made sense. *Oui* is French for *yeah* French is proof you are gooder at cooking than anybody else & when you shout *OUI!* it's kind of like promising that carrot tartare is genius & ten fifty is a handsome wage & cutting sunchokes on a bandsaw is fine & the chervil emulsion doesn't smell like hot puke & Chef never rubbed salt into your burn & King Chef doesn't not hire fat people & we don't throw out all of our perfectly good *mise en place* at the end of each day even pickles even oil-poached octopus from today & we believe Chef when he says he'd die for this restaurant & wood sorrel is a fashionable hat for any ingredient & these robes. are the most exquisite robes. we have all ever seen. these tailors. these genius tailors. --the finest silks--

LET'S HAVE A GOOD SERVICE

OUI!

Service Shift

I NEVER FELT I should be trusted walking about that dining room but no cook was exempt from the service shift and therefore once a week or month I had to run food to tables and tell our guests what the fuck we did to it back in the kitchen. Have you ever heard of that medieval torture method in which a rat in a bowl is tied to a person's belly then a torch is held up to the bowl until the rat burrows into the belly at a chance for survival. Well yes very nearly. On my first shift I knocked a lady's water on her lap ran away told the floor captain didn't know what table number could only say over there it is rude to point.

Service Shift II (Show Duck)

SO ONE DAY THIS lady and her husband were sitting at a two top all guests at twos sat adjacent to each other as they were paying to see us & not each other. I was on a service shift so I had to bring the duck course out to them but as soon as I got there the woman picked up her phone. The guy said wait so I stood there with my duck. I didn't mind waiting it was whatever but I do know a little Spanish which is what she was speaking so as I was holding this duck and waiting for her to finish her call I realized she was in the middle of learning her father had died. & so suddenly I had no fucking idea why I was holding this idiot copper sautoir with our duck which is dry aged for twenty-eight days rubbed with honey lavender and a few other spices roasted whole then sodomized with a bouquet of lavender before we hold it patiently in front of your face while you receive bad news on your phone facing the dining room & not each other. She was trapped hung up the phone urged me to complete my final performance the one she had likely waited months or maybe years to see she smiled politely through tears while I said this duck is dry aged for twenty-eight days rubbed with honey lavender and a few other spices roasted whole then we shove a bouquet of lavender up its ass for a little added charm. Well her phone call broke our eighth wall such that we just became two dioramas conjoined at faulty universe & suspended ghastly in the foldingness and unfurling of it all. We were alive and we were dying and we were trapped in this play or these two facing plays and we were too close to curtains to stop now so we just did our words with the mutual knowing that this was very fucked and very fucked and very fucked indeed.

Grocery Thief, etc.

IN POVERTY & DESIRE to once again thin myself I was frugal with eating miserly with money I ate green coffee cleanse pills and granola samples from Pret A Manger for breakfast snacked on scraps at work for lunch and dinner. But oh come night by the burn of wine or strong beer from the bar around the corner I escaped the cage of my exoskeleton something like quicksilver & got myself all over everything. As soon as I drank enough to detach from my skin I could see out my eyes without the peripheral smudge of self & everything I saw was mine. I went inward like the world was gone & I could just open a door to the inner pantry of my mind & descend into a lair of safety from restriction. A pleasure trove of want & get and I loved it I was perfect in those moments because I was blank of body & all mouth & the floating self knew only of temperature texture scent and flavor nothing was tinged with guilt or fear I was royal everything I touched I deserved I was wealthy in delight if I was standing in front of the open fridge it only felt like I was feeding from the depths of my iron-belted brain. Mornings of spilled wine bread shards smeary countertops & scrawled out bills for my roommate's stolen groceries & fuck she shopped at Citarella sixty dollars really. Yes really this girl was done with it she did not renew her lease she did not tell me in advance & I did not then have a place to live. Then again I also did not have a place to work as I had misplaced my tweezers & was thereby rendered obsolete

me and my hands oh offensive liaisons we took ourselves and quit
The World's Best Restaurant & onward & downward we went.

Jerz

BROKE & UNTETHERED I moved in with my parents befriended
the icy liter of Absolut that lived in their freezer drank out of solo
cups as they unpacked from their move across town into a new and
smaller house for empty nesters. How thick it poured when frozen
something like clear blood I hate vodka but sometimes opinions
wilt. I sat on the bed in their guest room looking for a job on
Craigslist doing anything other than cooking I resented the kitchen
it was so douchey & fluorescent the tickets tiles tape tweezers the
meanness the machinery of it the sterile cold metallic. But the
friction. Escape against stagnation & parents against blood-thick
vodka against me. I couldn't find another job my parents got tired
of me loafing about gloomy & mad at New Jersey & there was the
bus stop & here was my ten bucks & here was my backpack & there
was the Empire State Building you can see it from the highway as
you lurch toward the Lincoln. My friend offered me her temporarily
abandoned room in someone else's place & I took it, lack of bed be
damned, ninety-five degree August nights be damned, damn it all,
as I slunk back to kitchens, fresh out of escape plans.

Potatoes Inside Your Actual Shoe

I TOOK A JOB at a Bobby Flay restaurant for reasons I cannot explain & I can't even really explain what's shameful about it because really the answer is nothing but it is Bobby Flay but then also he's quite a bit more normal than you'd expect but either way I am hoping you know what I mean when I say I don't understand what the fuck I was thinking but I mean that in the nicest way possible. Anyway I didn't stay there very long not just because of the Flay thing but more so because there's just something kind of fucked about kitchens that do three or four hundred covers a night you have a way of ending up with potatoes in your shoe & no time to get them out it's all very shleppy slingy & somewhat desperate. Besides which I was tired of being put on garde manger/fry it was the fifth time in my life & didn't anyone feel like letting me near a pan. Just around the corner was my favorite restaurant in New York City & even though I'd had a bad feeling about shitting where I ate I had run out of ideas. It's true that food is food but you can't really just work anywhere you can lose your mind that way let me put it to you this way I once watched a sanitation worker outside a mall sweeping up giant yellow flowers & no trash at all & wouldn't you say that's a different type of clock out sigh from the one you do after a day of collecting dog shit and dirty needles. So finally one January afternoon I went over to the good place & did a trail and they hired me onto the grill & there I went to finally cook some goddamn food.

Laying Stone

THE CHEF THERE WAS good at cooking good at speeches too never made us say *oui* at the end of them never made us say shit. Not that there were many speeches we all got together once a month or so to do the cohesion but otherwise we just worked. One such meeting she told us this story said a guy walking into a city approached three different men all laying stone, asked them what they were doing. The first two said laying stone; the third said building a church. What she wanted was for us to be the third guy about it all & see beyond our stone-laying existences. Build a church build a church when you don't behead a speech with *oui!* that shit stalks your audience indefinitely. Somewhere in the universe its heart blinks open and closed. Awaits its reckoning.

Brown

THE FOOD WE SERVED was brown glorious brown however it was green when it was green red when it was red we had many colors we just didn't Adam and Eve it all with chervil & flowers & micros & what have you. & people always ask what was it like to work there what was it like what was it like usually I just say good because it's mean to tell the truth to happy people. What I don't say is how we let the food be enough when it left the oven, as it presented itself to the world. That we were not compelled to cover it up for shame, protect people from the infinitude of form. That for the better part of those years I felt possible too.

Biscuits

SIMULTANEOUSLY THOUGH THE BODY was running away from me I was in love again but this time with so much at once & though I'd spent the previous six months working out living off bread heels coffee alcohol and some cocaine I was coming back to life & that meant another fattening. I worked with other women who loved eating worked for a woman who loved feeding dated a woman with a roving and ferocious hunger. Food everywhere & our glowing giddiness of its stewardship. Or horniness or attractingness we were just magnetic with it all ourselves our livings our cookings and our eatings. No I did not seek the fattening no I did not like it either it was just another truth if you are sprinting around on twelve hour shifts are you not gonna hot-minute-self-sequester in the walk-in & eat a fistful of cheese or maybe some ham scraps & after work if the servers are buying drinks because the cooks are poor and they are rich & this is the only socialism we can do then are you not gonna eat the wings that appear after some rounds. Sometimes I threw up staff meal in the restaurant bathroom but it was kind of half hearted & it didn't quell the fattening. Maybe more than anything it was like cats molesting the quilt in the constant quest for milk nipple more a hope than a means to an end because eventually I was just fat & sort of had to just go about my life being the cat and looking for the milk nipple and having the anxiety that it wouldn't be there & it wouldn't be there & I would just keep being the cat kneading into the void like where did she go I'm fairly certain she's around here somewhere.

The Good Food

THE STAFF WAS ALLOWED to drink quite a lot of alcohol after work at that restaurant. Actually I think we were allowed one shift drink but what happened was more much more we drained so many bottles of Cava but I was not who started it. The chef got mad at times said alcohol is a tool not a crutch you don't just get a drink after service you are supposed to be brought *back up* by the drink after being rode hard & put away wet. On us this information was mainly lost we were just always on and what were we gonna do. We did try to be good sometimes one brunch service the bartender made juicy sparkles with gin for all the cooks & someone said I don't think that's a good idea so I just hid them all in my lowboy since I was in charge and drank them all which in hindsight is fucked but if you drink a gallon of cocktails and don't die maybe they were mostly water. & I don't mean to say all that happened there was drinking there was also the eating of the ham and cheese in the walk-in & also the the best cooking ever to be done. We cooked so good & the people came & if they were lost & only wanted lettuce and dry chicken we could tell them all the best but *goodbye* & there was even so much butter in the goddamn air that vegans couldn't really sit inside and consider themselves chaste at least not really really. Rabbits & veal breast & sweetbreads & marrow & buttered steaks & trout meunière & mushroom toast & anchovies & sardines & garlic & garlic & rawest garlic & shrimp toast & butter & butter

& wall-to-wall butter & omelette & oyster & powdered sugar & blue cheese toast with butter & butter & butter. & rösti.

Church Guy

EVER AFTER THE DAYS in that kitchen I tried to remember to be
that church guy even just a bit but jesus fuck is it hard to look at
oneself and see anything more than everyone else much less be able
to convince everyone else of your more-than-themness. & harder
yet when the burden of proof is on you. You will never walk into a
kitchen in a female body & be more than them. Unless maybe your
more-than-themness precedes you like you murdered for it in the
past & now your kill ghost looms before you all triple-dog-dare.
It doesn't matter how many scars how sharp the knife how much
grace strength knowledge how much talking or not talking youth
or age. There is just your dumb stupid lady body, hips against apron
strings, disqualifying & qualifying everything you do. The guest
will eat your food & thank the dumb stupid man bodies next to
you. & they will say you're welcome.

You Should Not Push Your Slower Friend Down to Save Yourself From the Bear

IS WHAT I READ online the other day in an article about how to safely get away from a bear. (To be funny?) the article suggested that even if a friendship seems to have run its course it's best not to use your friend as bait so that you may live longer. A pair of underwear from the day before once fell out of my work pants onto the kitchen floor at the The Best Restaurant In The World & I didn't admit they were mine but the thing is I was the only girl in the savory kitchen & back then I was in a time of occasional lace. Simple no problem I blamed it on the girls working pastry I even said *sluts* to prove I was serious. That seemed to work the sous chef just shrugged laughed picked them up with tongs and put them in the trash (we never use tongs for cooking in good restaurants just for picking up panties off the floor). The thing about pushing your friend down for the bears is that bears run. Either they will eat you too or they'll let you hang out and live with the bears but even in the case of the latter they're not gonna share the fucking honey. And do you want the honey anyway if you have to nod and laugh when they say yo that cunt pastry chef she just needs a good fisting, you know what I mean not a fucking a fisting & let's see how many times I can grab the pastry sous' tit before she says anything. Ha ha. That was your laugh. The more you laugh the less it sounds off-key.

If You Are Packing Vag You Could Walk Into a Kitchen Holding a Head on a Spike & the Prepubescent First Day Intern Would Tell You a Better Way to Show Off Your Bounty.

A WHILE BACK THIS sixteen year old boy (let's just call him Tony Danza for the sake of privacy) came from Italy for a one month *stage* at this restaurant where I was the sous chef. His mom knew the owner & it seemed that she was paying us to take her son away for the summer. Tony Danza showed up in all the glory of a teenager who'd never done his own laundry or anything for that matter he talked to himself sung to himself cursed at himself etc. The owner paid the head chef to board him & the report was that he only ate Oreos & almond milk. Allegedly Tony Danza told the chef he got a rash *eena-de-geenital-ayreah* because of a bad burger at a local bar. Or so the story went. All I know is Tony Danza was eager to remove me from my allegorical cave & taught me so much he said: *Haven't you ever heard of Michelin Stars before. I cooked at a Michelin-rated three star restaurant for two whole months. Why doesn't this place have a Michelin Star? Did you know you can make mayonnaise from scratch. Hollandaise is a very famous French sauce. Why is hake on the menu. In Italy we only serve hake in hospitals. Pasta can only touch a wooden board not steel. This is an Italian dish? Maaaybe in Sicily.* To Tony Danza I always said wow no I never heard that before you are not allowed to hit kids also you are not allowed to hit anyone. Once I tried to explain to him the importance of Hellmann's but that was a mistake so instead I began to develop this fantasy that if one day I was asked by a major publication where I learned to cook I would say I learned everything I know from a sixteen year old intern named Tony Danza so that if it got back to him he would believe it & be proud & thereby live inside a lie that I invented & while that isn't feminism per se it is some form of playing God which could be considered by extension a certain form of feminism.

PART III

Panties

MY WIFE AND I have scored seats in front of the fireplace for drinks at The Silly Moose. I'm the chef at The Silly Goose & this is our sister restaurant by the same owners. It's a fancy place all dim lamps dark wood sexy & expensive the bar seething absinthe-colored light. We don't usually come here but might as well considering we are on the inside after all & with my recent promotion there's some kind of celebration to be had. The owner sees us comes over to say hi I say hi he says hi & then kisses me on the forehead. Oh no is what my brain tells while it tallies my stature in the company against the truth which is that he may think of me like a daughter because he has two around my age. & is the head kiss about the daughters. Maybe he forgot I wasn't his daughter. I mean is it not about the daughters. Well he's not from America it is a very European thing he's a nice guy means well didn't charge us for anything it's just cultural he doesn't know about Biden's head kissing debacle and all that probably. I sip my martini. Does he kiss The Silly Moose's chef on the head. This is making a funny because the chef here is a man. Well why is it funny. Well a man doesn't kiss a man's head. Why. Is it the age thing like a dad hating his son into manhood no head kisses for you. No it is some sort of professional shit. The boundary of the man. We don't have that do we. Another sip & I don't know the answer & I wonder what they got The Silly Moose's chef for Christmas they got me a camisole and panties did they get him panties too. I laugh. Is it funny because of buying a man underwear or because I don't do panties. Maybe he only likes panties but got boxers & we can trade. Is it funny because they don't have a son. What kind of underwear does Dan wear. Dan Dan I always forget Dan's name because they call him Chef did you talk to Chef let's ask Chef I mean that is how he introduces himself Hi Everybody My Name Is Chef Dan. I know how that goes but is that what we are doing. If the owner called me chef I would say no thank you but he doesn't attempt the formality, now replaces it with a forehead kiss? What would it be to look like Dan I wonder everyone listens to him he is handsome the cliche Hollywood man-chef instagrammable AF and all that shit. & how much money does he make. & what did they get him for Christmas. & what would it be like to look like Dan, at least tall enough for the head kiss to require tippy toes?

At The Silly Goose

WE SERVE BRUNCH EVERY day and dinner on the weekends dinner is what I like best you see people are so boring by day always eat the same breakfast and lunch never want to ingest calories in broad daylight live in palm-drenching terror that the dressing on the side might spill into their salad before sunset but oh by night in the dim dusky horny of the wine & the candles & the desperate flailing toward the un-self-censored un-self-chaperoned holy hours of the weekend. In these fleeting minutes of joy guarded on either side by the deep moats of Friday's gloaming and Monday's dawn they will eat everything sometimes even lamb instead of chicken sometimes even pasta instead of kale sometimes even cheese sometimes even butter sometimes even dressed salad sometimes they even lay their allergies to rest people are much less bad at night on the weekends much less bad than usual. Sometimes they even get some cake.

Splinter

AT HOME I EAT whatever I want only there is some sort of shattered algorithm in my brain that decides what that might be & even though I stand sixty pounds heavier now than at my illest weight I haven't stopped thinking like I did only there's someone else in there playing devil's advocate. Condiments are safe, lettuce safe. Bread crusts but not the whole slice. A heel is god in goatskin. Cheese is scary but a must for goodness. All the farting veggies can be had forever. Puffed kamut you can do the gavage of it. But nothing is off limits never no not at all. Mainly I eat scraps or just standing at the open fridge so as not to know my total--the frame of a plate rings loud. My wife likes a place setting whereas do I even want the evidence of a greasy utensil on my chafing conscience. I have a loophole though which is the drinking which softens the panic of a feeding. What I like is to scrap scrounge & drink & scrap scrounge some more if it's needed to hike out the keel but my wife likes a square dinner cooked proper every night. Well if I drink enough I can eat a lot & I will never have to tell myself what I did. If the drinking comes then I can eat off a plate & the only weirdness is how fast I do it my wife says slow down but I want the big bites because the big bites are so much at once. I want the big bites & I love them & the fastness quells the naggy braying of the disgust. & if I am done & the panic kicks up & my shoulders get tight & I can no longer focus on the movie we're watching then I have another drink & it is all OK & it is true that this is not a decent system but socially speaking drinking is quite less offensive than puking or at least we have all agreed that by default this is so.

Going Places

MOST OF THE COOKS at The Goose are under the age of twenty some of them are fifteen sixteen years old most everyone has never worked before never cooked either some of them are good some of them are bad well my wife says aren't they all bad but what is a standard and for what reason do we really measure against it & for what reason & for what. I can't help getting slightly proud of them it gives me something to see them learn I get a tickle in the heart when they scrub down the table or don't break the aioli or work through the rush it is true I've got measured expectations but why set them high if only to refuse the occasional side grin. Anyway I'm just a hopeless romantic when it comes to competence & I get ahead of myself sometimes let on I'm impressed & the kids they say *well actually I'm planning on going to med school. No offense.* None taken as I stand here portioning ketchup which is not life or death or even somewhat interesting I do get it you know.

Sap

ONE OF THE TEENAGE cooks shrinks before my eyes over six months or so it is slow and imperceptible until one day she stands working in only her bones. Well maybe she's just small won't it be awkward if I ask her where she went but she's gone kind of quiet kind of stoned almost & what is there to say to a fifteen-year-old almost nothing is right. This one black winter morning I open the kitchen with her & she seems a bit tired kind of slow to move kind of thinking or something I say what's wrong she stares at me point blank so tired like giving up and isn't scared isn't talking at ketchup just says words I never said to anyone. I think back to the tunnel with no end the help that never comes the horse that never splits itself open sternum to pelvis never brushes its entrails to the side as if to say get in & I do not have a plan for what to say or do. I sit down on the counter & I say words about bodies and their unbearable clinginess & how I know about the tunnel I even for some reason tell this child I think I might be trans as if that somehow helps her (or me?). If I am the horse in this case. Get in. Is there enough room? No she says & lays down next to me. But here's the thing when you leave yourself ajar-- you are unable to meddle helpfully much less discern where the fault cracks mine from yours, sense just bleeds out while all the shame of prying floods the dark & all that's left to say is nothing because the words are hanging ripe & you are not a horse at all you are just a beetle in the amber. The our is not an action but a shared knowing of a certain type of pain and what it wants. So we just puzzle nine pans together in silence sling a brunch service & hardly speak of it again. Each day in the kitchen. Bruised and oozing hopes splatting down around us.

The Gram

*Sorry I'm late insane morning I was showing an influencer around The Moose super VIP//Damn that's so crazy//I **know** she has **a lot** of followers.* This is how it's done now audacity of linen black or tan sun hat pics of the food pics with the food hashtag life is best lived hashtag ten pounds underweight middle part pony freebies & likes dark wood & mixologists microgreens & lamps {leave the mouth out of this}. She's here to shoot the salad & she says *I want **you** to make **me** the **prettiest** salad you've ever made.* Me, I enjoy being spoken to like a four year old in my own kitchen & how many salads have I made in my life maybe six thousand well alright here we go. I set to work knowing I shall disappoint her immensely. Even lettuce is not beautiful enough for instagram you need the rainbow & the taste is irrelevant & that's why the captions are always last priority & incorrect. We do the soup next & she says how it's just red and there's no green & isn't there something I could do to just give it a little pop. I just say no thank you. The silence hangs ominous because I'm murdering our likes & don't give a shit. Likes are what we want & we like it when there's *engagement* on our posts which is why this girl is always making violent snuff films with our pastries. The Owner says people love it when she tears our shit apart they don't want croissants leading peaceful lives & nothing grabs them quite like sparagmos of a filled donut. In general I am speechless but keep waking up each morning & there isn't much I can do to stop it all. Once in a while I hide a soft boiled egg or something inside the pastries awaiting public execution to keep the photographer on her toes. Why should we not all enjoy the entertainment of sacrifice.

Mood Board

I SIT DOWN FOR a meeting & the owners hold up a foam core board & I want to laugh because it looks like high school but something is sinister. Pixelated print-outs glare white lady salads & I look away. The use of glue sticks means the purchasing of glue sticks which means this is an ambush in the first degree it is not a conversation but a presentation & I unhinge my jaw for the duration let it gape in case my soul wants to escape I wouldn't begrudge it that. *OVER THE LAST YEAR WE'VE LOST SOME BUSINESS WE NEED TO GO BACK TO BASICS WHAT PEOPLE WANT ARE THINGS THAT ARE VERY FAMILIAR SORRY YOU JUST FINISHED CHANGING THE WHOLE MENU BUT WE HAVE TO CHANGE IT AGAIN WHAT ABOUT A GRAIN BOWL & ALSO IT COULD BE GLUTEN FREE. QUINOA! QUINOA IS GLUTEN FREE & WHAT ABOUT SMOKED SALMON SHOULDN'T WE HAVE THE OPTION OF SMOKED SALMON AS AN ADD-ON OH & ALSO CHICKEN ADD CHICKEN BREAST & ALSO AVOCADO & AVOCADO TOAST & CHICKEN BREAST. VERY SIMPLE. I CAN GIVE YOU AN AMAZING RECIPE FOR SALAD DRESSING ALSO WE SHOULD STOP SERVING DINNER WHAT IF WE WERE JUST A DAYTIME ESTABLISHMENT.*

Third Floor

BEHIND THE CHAIR I sit in at the meeting is a large window that looks down over the parking lot from the third floor & the blood rippling in me says if you jump out you can fly or die & either is best. What would it take to break through the glass. The panes? I can imagine the glory of flattening. Acid muscles sing the song of impact and isn't the skull just a patient geode. I envision my funeral. Think of my eulogy but who would be brave enough to say what I know. The Pinterest collage (oh inescapable plank of oppression) would sit uninvited in the place of my picture, next to my casket. My wife would cry. My therapist would (maybe but probably not however this is my fantasy) say fucking bastards. A strange pastor who makes no sense since we are Jews would raise a match to the board & say *her life was not wasted in death but rather in the fetid mire of #brunch. Let us drink to her freedom!* But I don't crash through the window at all instead I say I agree with canceling dinner service. What I'd really like is to cancel the restaurant altogether or quit but I need the money & the fewer hours I'm here the less I will think about the third floor window to the parking lot or have to witness myself cooking avocado toast for a living.

Knife Guy

I TRADE MY PANTS in for shorts set my own knives in the back seat of my car & pick up one of the shitty ones we keep in the restaurant that gets sharpened every couple of weeks by a strange man we kind of think keeps people tied up in his basement. If ever we talk about him he shows up two seconds later like he heard us so we whisper the theories but when the knives feel pretty dull we say Knife Guy Knife Guy Knife Guy & then there he is. But don't worry about the hypothetical basement people if anything he probably cooks them elaborate feasts brushes their hair each day maybe the occasional tea party. One cook says do you think he dresses up like a baby and all & I say no I don't really think so I rather prefer to think he just considers himself at their service. Still I don't know if that is about me or about what I think he deserves hey look at us all just giving out the deservings of others playing god playing chef most importantly playing do you like to play with knives do you like dull or sharp.

Fryer Oil

I CHANGE TO THE basic-ass menu as requested & there is now nothing to do for prep & so it's the little things that bring me the most joy. The happiest day of my week is Friday when the fryer oil is new clear and thin and shit doesn't burn in a festering foam before cooking all the way through. It is true that I could change it twice a week but I don't want to I like the extreme improvement on my life outlook a drastic change can make plus the biodiesel company is trying to frame someone for stealing our fry oil from the drum outside & I would rather keep them on their toes there is no robber I just haven't dumped much oil this quarter there is a five thousand dollar bounty on the head of the oil thief.

Ender: Purpose

I HIDE AN OCTOPUS in the barista fridge next to the milk & no
one laughs. I hide a cabbage patch doll in the walk-in & no one
laughs & I hide myself in a giant shipping box next to the pass and
ring for service and then jump out at the servers & no one screams
no one laughs no one pisses their pants a bit. One of the cooks
figures out that the gluten-free chocolate-peanut cookie dough
looks a lot like poop with corn in it if you roll and coil it properly
& this too is a helpful way to stay alive. I don't say that these are my
last shots at making good on days spent slicing ham. But maybe it
is obvious–ham slicing being not so hopeful a task. I mean what
really is it after all slicing ham building a church—or actually—
remember Ender's Game—that bad sci-fi novel about a boy who
was taken to work for the government & he and the other children
in the government barracks just played video games in the nude all
day had fun chilled whatever pretty innocent. Ender was good at
video games & eventually beat the last level of the game & found
out he killed a real race of aliens & what is games & he became the
accidental posterchild for a galactic genocide. Sometimes down here
in the lobotomizing fluorescence of the basement kitchen it gets
so I don't even know if the food we're making is for anyone at all if
the sandwich really even is a sandwich why we make it who's the
enemy who's the friend where the plates go once they're whisked
upstairs. In the trash maybe they just bring them up and throw them
out or maybe they just beam them to space & does it matter did

it matter about the aliens. What of tricking a child into exploding a population into vacuum-tumbling shrapnel & what is the trick on us the leg work is all so mundane & was the stone-laying guy really deluded about the church or did he know what it was for did he know what Ender was actually up to & why didn't he warn him did Ender already know & if he did then what do I already know of deli slicer & ham & what is there to be done about it.

Leap Year

IT IS MARCH IST and I am dying on account of the leap year party we threw for the staff last night at which I drank too many beers and also shots because the creepy dishwasher who wears rain boots brought tequila so that people would talk to him & I did. On the way home from the party I fell asleep and woke up several times & didn't recognize my own wife who was driving & kept drifting off & waking up to this stranger taking me home. When we got home I passed out then woke up & puked & Bettina drew me a bath & I puked in it and cried & puked & cried and my cat came to visit me and that helped but not that much because I also begged Bettina to kill me. So it is March 1st & I am hungover as fuck but also less than I should be thanks to the puking. But the bathroom is worse for it & we will have to throw out the bath mat due to the redness of chorizo & my clothes are in the shower in a shameful smelly pile. It's my day off but I'm scheduled to interview a dishwasher and prepare an oatmeal tasting for one of the owners so I drive slowly to the restaurant. I come in & I am suffering & the cooks are laughing but nicely and I say I have to make goddamn fucking oatmeal because the owners aren't sure what my *interpretation of porridge* will be & I just sit in front of the grill on its low stainless steel table & the heat is good on my back & my knees are tired. The teenagers have a look on their faces but is it sympathy or empathy & I can't. I have no plan for the oatmeal & I wither a little, put some dried currants in a ramekin. I begin to boil some grains and oats they want it gluten free but all I have is wheatberries. The GM is hungover too and wants to leave this fucking place so she offers to go to the store & buys some millet. & I boil it & it's disgusting so I just make oats with wheatberries and quinoa it is ugly but I am drunk & it is goddamn fucking porridge. Ten passes & no one shows for the tasting. I am disintegrating & go puke in the bathroom that is grossly next to the line & a cook says did you puke do you feel better & the answer to that cancels out among itself. The dishwasher interview comes in & I talk to her & say nice things about the restaurant & try not to puke because creepy rain boots is leaving & this woman has submitted with her application a *2-page resume* in a *folder* that she *bought* & has listed dishwashing as a passion alongside caring for Icelandic horses. So I hire her & get her to leave in case I puke again & I decide the oatmeal tasting is a hoax & the cooks are alright so I leave to go meet my sister who is visiting from the city. When I get to the coffee shop I get a text that says I'm on my way for the oatmeal tasting & I say no so we shoot for Wednesday. The dishwasher will quit in 2 weeks but I don't know that & my sister isn't mean when I tell her my apartment is bad & puke ridden & she comes back there with me and does my dishes while I tend to the bathroom & wonder if I'm bad or good & avoid memory blotches of having given minors shots at the party & try not to think about what I'm doing waking up trashed and presenting *my interpretation of* oatmeal to the owners & try not to

think about my wife hating me & try not to think about my waste
of a self the purity of potential the filth of kinetic & later we sing
Alanis Morisette loud enough to upset the neighbors & I forget
how loathsome I am & that is a very fancy thing.

Shit Shooting

WE GO TO LUNCH & my sister asks if I think I may kill myself. She does it nicely which is to say coded enough that Bettina doesn't follow. I laugh & look at my spoon because what can I do. Saying no would be nice but I am a person who feels obligated to the truth. I take a spoonful of soup. I guess there are other answers like aren't we already dead--and haven't I died before time and again into shimmers of relativity? Or a simple yes which wouldn't do at all. What is not a topic for lunch is that I imagine it often, have a real cohesive notion & everything, fantasy though it is.

Picture a Mountain.

WHEN I PICTURE THE mountain it is close to the sky very very close. Well what I mean is not a lot of trees and no bullshit overhead. The weather is bright & my body at first looks like a stick figure that is disproportionately large for the mountain just sticking off. If you zoom in you'll notice the sky is not quite as grey as it originally seemed not really blue but also not exactly the blindingness of sun against fog. & I am not really a stick figure but just actually me. I would be on the mountain which is rocky & sparsely tufted with moss & I would be trapped in the gravitational smother against the upness of the inner balloon. Like a fish in a wooden sweater. So to shed the incessant downness I'd prepare myself to jump. At this point I could access that giddiness that lives in the gilding of terror. Tingling of that fresh blueness peeling through & I would prepare myself for a very high jump. Blood lung running start & and then I'd launch myself, arms to panic-colored sky, and I would fling up gone. It is true that this flinging relies on gravity giving up. Either altogether briefly or just in that one tube of my ascent--but we have all heard of stranger stories and nodded our heads yes so grant me my momentary glitch. Because what I think is that I would shoot right into a section of the galaxy where shit felt good all the time & not at all like cement & the dishwasher showed up to work every day & I built the church no the city & I never had to wonder if falling on a sharp knife with all the weight of my body would get me home for the day. I would be dead, but it would really be fine, because I would be so unquenchably free. And so it is not really fair to say either no or yes to this question, but as it is lunch, I just laugh & go to the bathroom because lying is bad & we need to head to our hike before it gets too dark.

PART IV: EPILOGUE

The Present Poetic

LINEN GUY IS HERE with the towels he's a pretty squirrely dude
actually to be accurate he's so awkward that his presence causes me
physical pain & so I try to keep things moving. When he hands me
the invoice & says *thanks Baby Doll* I write him his check without
explaining why a baby doll would never have a checkbook or knives
or an upright skeleton, etc. It is faster this way. This place is my
restaurant, which is another way I can tell I'm neither an infant nor
a toy, but that is also a reason why I don't have time to correct this
misperception. I am busy instead cranking out yards of sausages,
tucking veils of caul fat around crépinettes, funneling blood into
intestines, boiling snouts. The Owners is me. Yea, as I conjure the
beigest of menus, there is no one waiting in the wings, shepherd's
crook poised, to snatch me and drop curtains. My chest freezer is
full of heads, feet, and fat, & I (to my own relative shock) seem to
vend those items with ease to an otherwise juice-cleansed society;
no one asks for chicken breast, no one asks for avo toast, no one
asks for egg whites. I feel joy in my heart when the newest batch of
bologna curls high off the griddle, joy when the pâté has slept for
long enough & slices true, joy when the trotters squinch suckingly
out of their chilled pot of jus. Sometimes the bologna fries flat.
Sometimes the pâté crumbles. Sometimes the trotter steps silently
into the world. & in these lesser moments, which some might refer
to as failures, as I stand stripped of my little victories, knee-deep in

my own mortality, I am at least certain, most very certain indeed, that I am not a baby doll.

CPSIA information can be obtained
at www.ICGtesting.com
Printed in the USA
BVHW070117211022
649943BV00003B/192